POETRY
BY
Simon

VOLUME 3

GOD'S BLESSING
MY JAMAICAN "GEM"

ROY LEE "SIMON" JARMON

Poetry By Simon

Volume 3

God's Blessing
My Jamaican "Gem"

Roy Lee "Simon" Jarmon

ISBN: 978-1-967375-00-4 (Paperback)
ISBN: 978-1-967375-01-1 (eBook)

Library of Congress Control Number: 2025907510

Printed in the United States of America

Published by:

info@thequippyquill.com
(302) 295-2278

CONTENTS

HEALING WOUNDS – INSPIRATION, COPING, AND RECOVERY

LOVE, ROMANCE, AND SUCH

Disclaimer

These writings are expressions formulated from my own thoughts, opinions, and fantasies that I have acquired during my lifetime. I have used many names in my writings; however, these names do not reflect the true identity of any particular person or individual unless specifically stated. The names used by me are for rhythmic, iambic, and/or poetic reasons only and do not apply to any particular or specific person, place, or thing.

Dedication

I promised God that all my books and all else that I do will be dedicated to him. Nonetheless, in this book, I want to thank and acknowledge my wife, Audrey Diane-Faye Yvonne Hines, who encourages me every day to continue my writings because of their ability to encourage and uplift, and inspire others. I also appreciate her for being my crutch that steadies me when I stumble as I stagger out of my comfort zone.

Audrey is a descendant of Jamaican parents—the late Vincent Harold Hines and the late Hyacinth Hope (Salkey) Hines. She is the sibling of a younger sister and four brothers—one deceased—that was born from this union. She now works as the executive assistant to her third Chief Judge of the Newark Municipal Court in Newark, New Jersey.

Audrey is devout and steadfast in her religion and conviction. She is a petite and gorgeous woman with a gigantic heart to support, encourage, and console others, especially hurting and/or abused women.

I don't know what her father had in mind when he nicknamed her Gem. Nonetheless, she is a gem in so many different aspects to quite a variety of people. Yes, she's a brilliant gem of a woman, especially to me as my wife, friend, and confidant. To that I say, "To God be the Glory for placing her into my life!"

Acknowledgments

To Bernice Frinch, I believe that I failed to mention your name in my book Poetry by Simon: Volume 2; Circle of Life—the Vershelle Cato Experience.

To LaReatha Payne, I believe that I misspelled your name in my book Poetry by Simon: Volume 2; Circle of Life—the Vershelle Cato Experience.

Special thanks and acknowledgment to the members of my church (HCF—Hallelujah Christian Fellowship Ministries) for their many prayers and encouraging words of support. God's great man of integrity shepherds HCF Ministries: our senior pastor, Bishop Eddie Bennett Jr., and his wife (our prophetic First Lady), Dr. Yvonne M. Bennett. Thank God for such wonderful leaders. Please, God, continue to bless them and keep them covered. Amen! Thanks again, you guys! And to God be the glory!

SPOUSE, FRIENDS, AND FAMILY
DEDICATION

My Wedding Vows

(From Roy to Audrey on our wedding day on November 7, 2009)

These words that I am going to say are sometimes spoken of as vows. They wrote their own vows, some may say. However, these are not my vows to you; God wrote my vows to you in his Holy Scriptures over two thousand years ago. These words are instead a testament of God's great blessing that can be bestowed upon one when he decides to allow the master to guide his steps.

So, to you, Audrey, this waiting congregation, and to the world, here goes:

Audrey, the day before I met you, I felt like a deflated basketball that had been lost in a field of high, overgrown weeds. I had no air in my tubes of life. I felt lost, listless, and confused. I felt—it seemed

—that I had no purpose.

Audrey, my dear, the day before I met you, I felt like a no-longer-used rowboat that was tied to the shore during rough, high tide in a constant, raging storm. I was tossed and thrown to and fro, up and down, left and right, back and forward by the angry waves of indecision and complacency. I had—it seemed—no direction.

Audrey, my love, on the day before I met you, I felt like a fragile twig that had fallen from a decaying tree into a swiftly flowing stream, twisting, tumbling, floating at the mercy of the stream's current with no place, no peace, and no destiny of my own.

But God ...

But since I've met you, this old basketball has had the air of life breathed back into its lungs of life. The weeds of confusion are mowed down, and I am bouncing back into the game of living again. And my purpose is to love you as deeply and as tenderly as Christ has loved his church.

Not So Long Ago

(Written to Audrey)

Not so long ago, I piddled throughout the night—
    Not thinking about going to bed—
    Let alone trying to go to sleep.
Not so long ago, I would not dare to step outside my house of
confinement.
    It was like crawling out of the ocean
    When you have become accustomed to living in the deep.
Not so long ago, I made it my business to shy away from the outside
world.
    I could not let them know that I was a crier:
    Sometimes I would really weep.
Not so long ago, I stayed only in my own little corner of this world.
    And when I did attempt to venture out,
    I would feel like I was a creep.
Not so long ago, to imagine that I could feel this way—
    Confident and eager to go forward—
    Was more than a quantum leap.
But that was before I met you, Audrey.
    And now, your angelic presence constantly plants the
    Pitter-patter thoughts of you
    In my mind day and night.
But that was before I met you, Audrey.
    And now, you have become the goddess of my soul.
But that was before I met you, Audrey.
    And now, you have become the queen of my heart.
Yes, not so long ago, Audrey, you made me begin to feel unafraid
    To live again. And now I feel alive—like being reborn.
    And that's a feeling that I want to keep.
    Thank you, Audrey.
Thank God for you!

Audrey's Whammy

(Written for Audrey)

YOU PUT THE WHAMMY ON ME!
    I was inclined to meet you without any reservations.
    Now I want to run to you without any hesitation.
YOU PUT THE WHAMMY ON ME!

YOU PUT THE WHAMMY ON ME!
    The aurora of your presence penetrated into my pores.
    And I find myself, daily, singing, "Darling, make me yours."
YOU PUT THE WHAMMY ON ME!

YOU PUT THE WHAMMY ON ME!
    The first time that I looked into your beautiful brown eyes,
    I knew that I was hooked. I knew that I was hypnotized.
YOU PUT THE WHAMMY ON ME!

YOU PUT THE WHAMMY ON ME!
    The taste of your sweetness from your hot, passionate kiss
    Zapped my soul of all its strength, leaving me none to resist.
YOU PUT THE WHAMMY ON ME!

YOU PUT THE WHAMMY ON ME!
    You took control of my mind with your innocence and quiet charms.
    You rapidly swept me off my feet and landed me softly in your arms.
YOU PUT THE WHAMMY ON ME!

YOU PUT THE WHAMMY ON ME!
    My thoughts of you are in my mind every night and every day.
    How crushed, deflated, and rejected I would feel if you ever went away.
YOU PUT THE WHAMMY ON ME!

YOU PUT THE WHAMMY ON ME!
    You have captured the heart of this old, overweight man
    And changed my life's outlook: I feel like living again.
YOU PUT THE WHAMMY ON ME!

My Love for You

(A poem written to Audrey)

I fell so deep
and I fell so fast
that I said our love was wrong.

But I think that
it's only because
my love for you is so strong.

When I'm entwined
in your loving arms,
I feel that's where I belong.

For you have made
my lifeless heart sing:
and it's singing a happy song.

To My Dearest and Beloved Wife

(Written to "my God's gift from above," Audrey, for Mother's Day)

My first thought was to write you a gushing,
Hot, passionate letter of love.
I was to pinpoint, pick out, project, and parlay
Your obvious traits and, shall I say,
Your beautiful, gorgeous, sexy, and voluptuous attributes.

Oh yes, I was to opine
The sublime
With rhythm and rhyme.
I was to lay it on thick
With passion and persuasion.
To make you gush!
To make you blush!
To make you hot!
But still don't stop
Until you sweat—but yet!

As I began to pen this letter,
My spirit did me one worse—
I mean better!
As I was pondering,
My mind was wondering
And my heart began to burn.
It came from deep inside of me,
Jumped on my back, and began to ride me—
Which in itself was a menial task
Until I realized what my spirit had asked.
It said, "Roy, my son, my boy,
As a husband, a man, and a lover,
What have you learned?"

So there lay my heart: prone,
Wide-open, and free,
Waiting on the timeless one,
Waiting for him to reach me.

Begging that his almighty wisdom
That he has housed since the eaves of time
Would teach me.
And he said to me,
"This is my daughter, so treat her right.
There's much more beyond a passionate night.
That's only the start of another day
On the journey of love! Oh, by the way,
Love is not a destination pursued by one
But it's a forever journey that's never done.
So as your passionate night
Lays you out to rest,
Make sure that your heart knows
That this was not a conquest
But a sharing of two souls that belong to me.
And I designed this meeting
Way back in eternity!
And as your two souls melt
And dissolve into one,
Give thanks to me,
Her Heavenly Father, my son."
So every day that he gives me life
And allows me to open my eyes,
I thank him for you, my wonderful wife.
Don't you think that's wise?
So on my knees, I praise and thank him
For remembering and blessing his son, Roy.
And I look forward to—
If my heart can stand it—
A little more of your love
And a lot more of your joy!

Happy Mother's Day, my dear!

(I've Found) A Good Thing

He who finds a wife finds a good thing, and obtains favor from the Lord.

—Prov. 18:22, NKJV

It states that he who finds a wife. It doesn't say a girlfriend, a lady, or a woman, but a wife. I know of many men who are married, but they really don't have a wife. She's just a female whom he has married. So check the scriptures and learn about the characteristics of a wife.

I remember once upon a time,
And it was not very long ago,
My life was going around in circles—
Sometimes fast, sometimes slow.
It seemed that I could not change my direction,
Like a bird with a broken wing.
Then God brought Audrey into my life,
And I found a *good thing!*

And then there were these circumstances
That controlled my day and my night.
Something would come and push me left,
And then something else would push me right.
I was dangling all over the place—
Like a puppet hanging from a string.
Then God brought Audrey into my life,
And I found a *good thing*!

Through meeting her and knowing God,
My life began to stabilize.
Having faith and trusting in him,
I was finally able to open my eyes.
As we prayed together—I was on my knees—
I offered and she accepted my ring.
God brought me Audrey and made her my wife,
And I have found a *good thing*!

2010 Valentine's Day

(Written to my wife, Audrey, on the Valentine's Day card sent to her office with the bouquet of flowers that I had the florist deliver)

My dearest wife, Audrey,

Beautiful flowers
For a beautiful lady
Is being sent your way
In hopes that it
Will lift your spirits
On this Valentine's Day.

But don't let it
Lift your spirits
To the point that you might roam,
Because it's only
A prelude to
What's waiting for you at home.

Your loving husband,
Roy

To Rohan

(Written in response to Rohan Lockhart Daire's—Audrey's youngest son—retirement party from the CTDOC [Connecticut Department of Corrections]. Read to him and his family on the following morning at his home.)

Rohan Lockhart Daire! Wait! Let me get this right. To Mr. Lt. Rohan Lockhart Daire, let me begin by saying, "Congratulations on achieving such a great milestone in your life!" You have accomplished an endeavor that many have not and many have attempted and failed. You have completed a task of high honor, of which you should be proud.

Our paths crossed only a few years ago, but to me, it seems that we've always been family. And I can say that because it's the type of person that you are. I have found you to be a person of integrity. You are a man of your word. You don't like to put up with a lot of— let me just say— "stuff."

When I first met you through your mother and observed your large physique, I said to myself, "I sure don't want him to get hold of me." Your big arms could probably put me in a headlock and easily break my neck or burst my head like a dropped watermelon on concrete pavement. You got huge biceps like Hulk Hogan. You got some powerful pecs under that shirt. And you got big, broad
shoulders to lean on.

But do you know what, Rohan? Lieutenant Daire? And I've seen it. I'm sure that others have seen it too. Do you know what your biggest muscle is? Your biggest and strongest muscle is your heart!

You care about people. You would rather talk to a person than talk about that person. You want to lift people instead of putting someone down. You are willing to walk step-by-step with a person instead of stepping on a person. Yes, you are a big, powerful, muscular man, but you are made so much bigger by having such a big heart.

So you should not be surprised that people want to be around you, because you are a good example of a man with whom to keep company. You should not be surprised when you see all types of heads popping from around corners and the many faces peeping through windows, because you are a good example of a man to watch and emulate when one wants to get ahead.

And don't be surprised when you look over your shoulder or when you look behind you and see numerous people who are trying to walk in your footsteps, because you are a good example of a man to follow.

Again, we are proud of your accomplishments, and we love you very much! But one more thing ...

I know that you are a man's man. A macho man, so to speak. You don't care—so you say—about all that mushy stuff, especially in public. But I have a little poem for you.

Now it's not about you. It's about others' relationship to you. It's about the impact that you've had on them and their lives. It's called "Learn to Say Goodbye."

I wrote it a while ago, but I'm sure that I can make it fit this occasion with a few word changes. So here it goes.

Learn to Say Goodbye

When I was a small boy, I saw on TV
A very touching story that's still with me.
While watching the story, I began to cry.
The story was called "Learn to Say Goodbye."

I've told this story from time to time
To ease the pain in friends of mine.
I've used the expression when people ask why.
I say, "Everyone must learn to say goodbye."

We'll all have heartaches as sure as we're born.
We'll all someday need a shoulder to lean on.
So I've used that expression sometimes as a crutch
When a person has lost someone they love so much.

Now we must say goodbye somehow, someday.
Lieutenant Daire is leaving us. He is going away.
Can we get through this? We will we pray.
But we'd sure like to see him come back and stay.

So God bless you, my brother, in all your future endeavors. To God be the glory!

Thanksgiving
by
Audrey "Gem" Hines Jarmon

It's Thanksgiving,
And now here comes the kids.
Panic sets in
Because of their demands
Of what they want
For breakfast, lunch, and dinner.

Of course, what do I do?
I get centered,
Run to the store and
Spend cash
That I would rather spend
On shoes and clothes.

But oh!
A reminder!
It's for the kids.
It's time for a family get-together.
I get it.
So I settled down
And did it all
With mixed emotions
Overridden by joy and thankfulness.

Cooking through until the morning,
I enjoyed every minute of it.
Watching the smiling faces
As they chewed down on
Their favorite dish, and
That was good enough for me.

DAILY "SLICES OF LIFE'S" EXCURSIONS

At the Gym

I was at the gym the other day, and there was this guy there—full of flab. His skin was flabby as could be. Don't mention those cottage cheese legs he had. "Wow! Look at that!" I said to myself as I thought, He should be ashamed of himself.

And there was this lady with the biggest ... uh, uh ... behind and thighs that I had ever seen. And I mean huge! You could count the dimples through her sweats. "Wow! Look at that!" I said to myself as I thought, *She should be ashamed of herself.*

And this old man's stomach was gigantic. He looked like he was twelve months pregnant with triplets. He looked as if he would burst wide-open at any minute. "Wow! Look at that!" I said to myself as I thought, *He should be ashamed of himself.*

And there was this young lady with her double—no, I mean triple—chin. She was fat from feet to head. My! What a fat face. She is too young to be that fat in the face. Her sweat looked like grease oozing from her pores. "Wow! Look at that!" I said to myself as I thought, *She should be ashamed of herself.*

So I finished my workout routine and made my way to the men's locker room. I gathered my towel and toiletries and headed to the showers. On my way, I passed the mirror and happened to notice a man with a flabby chest and oversized gut, who was flapping and giggling. He had a double chin and cottage cheese thighs. "Wow, look at that!" I said to myself as I thought, *Man, I should be ashamed of myself.*

Connections

Sun rises.
Sun sets.
Desert dries.
Water wets.
Connections!?

Baby awakes.
Baby cries.
Baby lives.
Baby dies.
Connections!?

It happens here.
It happens there:
Over yonder
And everywhere.
Connections!?

The same differences—
These rejections.
The same differences—
These connections.
Connections!?

In Reply to Judge Victoria

(My reply written in response to her congratulatory card that she sent me for my entry into the Veterans Affairs creative writing contest that was held at Lyons, New Jersey, Veterans Affairs Health Care Center)

My Dearest, Your Honorable Victoria Pratt:

I received your card of thanks!
When I realized that it was from you,
My heart pounded with anticipation.
And I knew that it was just one sheet withdrawn
From your overflowing vessel of honest integrity
Without any reciprocal expectation.
Thanks for your words of encouragement.
I shall go forward with the power of
Your humbly expressed recommendation.
I have certainly found it a blessing to have met you.
May God continue to bless you as
I express my heartfelt appreciation.

Forever grateful,
Roy Jarmon

I Am So Proud of You

(This poem was written while entertaining the thought of Judge Victoria Pratt being appointed as the chief judge of the Newark Municipal Court, New Jersey.)

I understand that congratulations is in order,
Even though some have attempted to beat you black and blue.
But with God by your side, I see that you have overcome.
I am so proud of you.

I'm sure that there was a long list of names
Of which many were deserving and well overdue.
But occupying that chair is whom God has chosen.
I am so proud of you.

Some may say that you were the dark horse in the race

When in actuality, you were not racing at all.
You were merely grazing in God's green pasture
When he decided to give you the call.

So now that you are chosen and have accepted the call,

Just go forward and do what you do.
No weapon formed against you shall prosper
Because I—no, God is proud of you.

So congratulations on your new position. Go with God and be blessed and be a blessing to all.

The Grip

"From whence did it come?"
Reality?
It bugged.
I tugged.
I scratched.
It snatched me.
The grip had hold
Of me—being bold
I pulled.
It tightened.
I sighed.
It cut.
I cried,
"The hurt!"
It tore.
The pain!
"No more!"
I couldn't escape.
The pain was too great.
"Help!" I yelled.
No one hope.
I tried to cope.
It tightened like hell.
I then collapsed,
And the grip fell.

The Watchers

We, my family and I, lived next to the levee that snaked itself alongside the Mississippi River. Refuge, the plantation on which we lived, was the first stop off at the foot of the bridge as one crossed from Arkansas into Mississippi.

Our houses—shacks—were along a turnrow (road throughout the plantation that provided a pathway to move and transport tractors and other machines to different fields) that ran almost parallel to the levee.

While I thought that I knew quite a bit about the KKK, I never knew—until I was fully grown—how much we were sheltered (protected) from them by our parents and others.

I can recall, during my early teen and preteen years, Dad and the other neighborhood men performed certain rituals in which we were not privy to understand the nature of their full benefit.

Dad would spend quite some time polishing, cleaning, and oiling every weapon (gun) in the house—that old pistol that looked like it was from the Civil War era; the old double-barrel shotgun with duct tape wrapped around the stock to hold the wooden part of the handle in place; and the dusty old .22 rifle that I'd seen in the corner of the closet for some many years. Yes, he would be up until late hours at night, preparing the guns.

And then the night would arrive. There would be big bonfires on the levee. We were told to turn out all the lights (or lamps and blow out all the candles) and to stay in the house. There would be a pile of old guns leaning against the porch, waiting for their turn, if need be. The black men patrolled the area back and forth down the turnrows. They were careful to look underneath and behind the houses. They also kept watch around the hog pen and chicken coops to make sure that no one was hiding there. All the houses would be pitch dark. The men walked while they talked strategies if the worst would occur. All of us kids were on our knees with our chins on the windowsill, peering out into the darkness and wondering what was going on.

Mom, through her nervousness, would sometimes say, "You kids get out that window."

"What's going on, Ma?" we would ask. "Why are they walking around out there in the dark?"

"You just get out that window and be quiet. You never know what can happen. Y'all need to be in the bed anyway."

It wasn't until many years later that I found out that the fires on the levee were the KKK having their monthly cross-burning meetings. And the men were prancing outside just in case they would decide to go on one of their hunting sprees, so to speak.

To this day, I thank God that—in those situations—we were spared from their hunting sprees in our area. We would often hear of situations on other plantations, but Refuge Plantation (where we lived) never had any of those raids. I had always thought that we were spared because of our men patrolling outside. But I think I heard Daddy or one of the men (and I'm quite sure that I did) slip one time and highly suggested that Refuge Plantation was owned by the grand master himself. Wow!

Instead of calling this piece "The Watchers," I could have entitled it "Living in Enemy Territory." I guess I couldn't say that I was glad we lived on the grand master's plantation, but I sure am glad that they didn't go hunting in my neck of the woods.

Two Men Kissing

He saw him amid the crowd from twenty yards away. His heart began to flutter. His heart began to beat faster and faster and faster.

Oh, how he longed to see him again. To hold him in his arms again. To hug and squeeze him again.

Thank God, he decided to come back. Their last meeting was a little hectic. Quite heated. Actually, they were quite rude and offensive toward each other. They had argued quite vociferously.

However, he reached out over the long miles—the vast distance—with a heart full of love but heavy with guilt and loneliness. And he was certainly glad that he did because they both realized that they did love each other deeply, and they wanted that love to thrive and grow. They knew that apart they were just two heartbroken men, but together they were a force and shield for each other for generations to come.

His distance was closer now, and he looked up and spotted him jumping up and down, waving frantically and yelling at the top of his lungs. They both ran toward each other as fast as they could.

And then they met. He jumped into his arms, and he hugged him so tightly that one could see the strains of every muscle, tendon, and sinew in his arms. They both were ecstatic to see each other again and to be in each other's arms. They both had tears of joy pouring from their eyes, and deep-throated grunts leaped from their mouths.

He firmly placed his hands on both sides of his head and pulled— with almost a strong snatch—his face toward him. He kissed him tenderly on his forehead. Then affectionately on the tip of his nose. And then on his lips, which were wetly saturated with his tears.

They hugged tightly again and then started walking—shoulder to shoulder—toward the baggage claim area with their arms around each other's back and waist.

Their eyes were red and swollen from crying buckets of joyful tears. Their lips trembled with excitement as they began searching the conveyer belt for his luggage.

My god, isn't it a beautiful and wonderful sight when father and son come together on one accord?

Was I Right?

(A healthy relationship doesn't just happen; it takes work. There are many decisions that one must consider. Here is one.)

"I thought you heated that piece of pie for both of us to share. But you went and ate the whole thing," she said.

"But I kept asking you whether to warm you a slice or not. I kept asking, and you just ignored me," I said as I ran the water and dishwashing soap in the sink, preparing to wash the dishes and utensils in my hands.

"Yes, I was on the phone, so ..." she stated as she cut herself a piece of apple crumb pie and placed it in the microwave oven to heat it.

I had plenty of suds and warm water by now and was washing away. There were only a few dishes, spoons, forks, and knives to wash. So I proceeded washing while this thought formulated in my mind: After I finish washing these dishes and she has finished her pie, I'll approach her and say, "My dear, I'm sorry about eating the whole piece of pie. I apologize, but I feel that we need to communicate a little better. I try and show patience, and I feel that sometimes you ignore me. I ask for information and get what I feel are partial answers or answers to some other question that I didn't ask. So often I speak to you and get no response at all, neither yea nor nay. Don't let you get on a roll, I'm ignored totally. Sweetheart, I just want us to communicate more openly and truthfully. I just want to feel included, that's all."

So now I was ready. I'd washed and rinsed all the dishes and placed them into the drying rack. I'd wiped the countertop. I was cleaning and rinsing the sink when she came over with her empty saucer. I dried my hands on the towel and took the dish from her with my left hand. At the same time, I gently reached and took hold of her arm as she was turning to walk away. She whirled to face me, and we automatically walked into each other's arms. We embraced. We hugged each other tightly—for quite a while (I might add)—and made heartfelt, soothing, hugging utterances.

It felt as if we were melting into each other and becoming one. And with that, all my previous thoughts and feelings of neglect melted away too. So I never said a word about what I was thinking and feeling earlier. Was I right?

It really isn't a big problem anyway, I thought. I felt that God had really blessed me abundantly with someone whom I know really loves me and someone who is so easy to love, someone who encourages me, someone who makes me very happy. So why do these few moments of insecurity or neglect arise? I don't know, and I think that I'm all right. I'm okay. But was I right not to say anything?

I'm fine now. Those feelings don't linger. They pop up once in a while but soon dissipate. I'm sure that it's something that I can live with. Something that I can tolerate. But I ask you, was I right not to say a word? Right now I'm fine, and I'm sure that I will always be fine with it. But was I right? What do you think? Tell me! Was I right not to say a word about my thoughts?

Man Cannot Make a Coconut

You can decorate it. You can grow it.
You can catch it.
You can throw it.
You can eat it.
You can bake it.
You can plant it.
But you cannot make it.

You can plant an okra seed
But you can't make the pod.
We call it a black walnut
And it has the hardest shell that I've ever seen.
Sure, it's black when it's finished
But did you know that it started out green?

We can accomplish extraordinary feats
As inventions and discoveries unravel.
We can realize amazing knowledge
As through earth, ocean, and space we travel.
Yes, there are many things that we can do
On this journey of life we trod.
But we must realize our limitations
And leave certain things to God.

The Number or the Button (Take a Second Look)

The scriptures say that we should hate the sin but not the person. However, when we look at it humanly, they seem to be the same— the sinner and the sin, that is. Humanly, it's quite difficult to separate the two, especially when you feel that the sin is directed toward you. Let's say a slap to your left check (a slap in the face). Slap!

Now how do you—how do I—separate that slap from the slapper? How? Can you? Do you? My, my, my! What a question. We can't slap the slap because that would mean that we are slapping ourselves. So who's left? Nobody but the slapper.

Yes, we end up slapping the slapper, and that's where we go wrong. Where? Where? Why is that wrong? Why is that wrong? Because we are not supposed to slap back. (Oh, I like that sound— slap back. We could do something with t

hat (slap back), but maybe later.)

We are to turn the other cheek. Ha! Sure we are. If we want to utilize one scripture, then we must utilize all of them. I think that's how we must look at the situation.

There is a person, a body, a temple. Within that person, that body, that temple lives, let's say, a spirit. That spirit controls everything that happens within that person, that body, that temple. Now I didn't say whether that spirit is good or evil. It doesn't matter. I humanly can't do a thing with, to, nor about that spirit. But I do know a spirit that can.

See, that person, that body, that temple can be an old, falling- down shack that's nearly lost and hidden in desolate woods. Or that person, that body, that temple can be an elegant, glamorous, high- class, well-lit mansion that sits on the hill. It's who lives inside of that person, that body, that temple that counts. And even more important still is the spirit that resides or lives within that controls and conducts your actions and reactions. Who is the spirit that lies in you, your body, your temple?

Yes, I know that it's hard to separate, let's just say, one from the other. No, on second thought, we better stay on point and say it: the sin from the sinner. And that's what we must do from time to time. Take a second thought. We may discover something about ourselves. To wit, who lives within me, my body, my temple.

We were on a trip, and we were in this beautiful, elegant, upscale hotel. Even the elevator was gorgeous. In the elevator, you had to push a certain button to get you to where you wanted to go. On the wall of the elevator were these beautiful, shiny golden numbers. Right beside each number was a beautiful, shiny round silver button. And every time that I got into the elevator, I would push that beautiful, shiny golden number. Do you know what happened every time I pushed that beautiful, shiny golden number? Nothing! Yes, nothing! I said, "What's going on here?" And then I took a second thought. Oh, now I see. Instead of pushing the beautiful, shiny golden number, I needed to push the beautiful, shiny round silver button. And when I pushed the beautiful, shiny round silver button, it lit up and the elevator began to move.

Aha! The numbers revealed where we wanted to go, but it was the button that caused it all to happen.

The person, the body, the temple are—shall we say, in a manner of speaking—separate, though somewhat the same, from the spirit, as the beautiful, shiny golden numbers are separate from the beautiful, shiny round silver buttons even though they are still tied together. They are linked to each other. They define each other. But they are (when it comes right down to it) their own separate entities.

And oftentimes, we go through life not taking a second look. We just react through frustration. And when that doesn't work, we get even more frustrated. The next time that the elevator doesn't move in your life, stop! Take a second look. See if you are pushing the beautiful, shiny golden number instead of the beautiful, shiny round silver button.

Are you concentrating more on the person, the body, or the temple than on the spirit that lives within? Let's take a second look at ourselves. Are we pushing all the numbers and still getting nowhere instead of pushing the button that's linked to the number? Let's take a second look at others and, most of all, ourselves.

Your Human Is Showing

When people write, when people phone,
And when people come together,
Guess what subject always comes up.
You're right! It's the weather.

"It's really hot!" or "Today's a scorcher!"
You might hear someone say.
And this summer they told the truth.
I wiped sweat every day.

It's still summer, and days are still hot,
But no fans are running tonight.
Suddenly the temperature dropped, and
No one's fussing about the heat from the light.

Now they're saying, "Gosh, it's cold!" and
"I wonder what made the weather change."
They want it neither hot nor cold.
I guess they just want to complain.

The Seventh Apple

Man, that was the sweetest and juiciest apple that I have eaten in a long, long time. Really, I'm not sure that I've ever tasted an apple as sweet as that one.

On my first bite into it—I wasn't prepared for this—the juice splattered, skeeted, and flew all over the place. On that first crunching sound of my first bite, the juice flew into my mouth, splattered on my glasses, and skeeted on my chin and shirt. Mmmm! Sweet! Juicy!

Mind you, I was pulling away from the stop sign of the store's parking lot onto the street. See, I had stopped at the store to get two items—count them, two. I wanted to get some vitamins from the pharmacy and uh ... something else. I don't remember the other item right now, but I had made up my mind that from now on, I'm going to only get what's on my list. You know how it is, don't you? You go in there—in the store. "Oh, wow! Look at this. I need one of those." And when you leave the store, you have a shopping cart full of everything except what you went there for. "Not this time," I said. So I didn't even get a cart. Not even one of those little hand-carry baskets.

I showed the greeter my membership card and headed straight toward the pharmacy. Before I had taken ten steps, there they were. Lo and behold, there they were—stacks and piles of plastic bags of the prettiest, mouthwatering-looking apples that I had ever seen. Oh, sooo enticing. They were right there in the aisle. You couldn't miss them. And you could see that they had just opened the huge cardboard box that they were shipped in. That meant fresh. Mmmm! Fresh, pretty, enticing, delicious red apples.

So as I was leaving the store, I saw him out of the peripheral of my left eye. I tried not to look in his direction. I tried turning my head to my right to avoid him, but it was like some invisible force prevented me. So then I tried to look down toward the ground, as I attempted to walk faster toward the car in the parking lot, but that didn't work either. Whatever that force was, it literally twisted my head—almost with a jerk—to my left.

There I was. Forced to face what I tried so hard to avoid. I was facing him, and my eyes latched on to his eyes—like a laser missile lock—as he slowly limped toward me, my cart, and my apples.

I know you caught it. I said that I didn't get a cart. Well, I didn't— at first. But I was so drawn to those pretty, juicy-looking apples that I did an about-face and ran to the entrance to grab me a shopping cart for my apples. I was compelled by that fruit, and I hurried back to the front and grabbed me a cart to put my apples in. Wow! Those apples were enticing. I'll bet Eve (in the Bible) knew how I felt.

Anyhow, while our eyes were locked on each other's, like a laser beam, I noticed him in a little more detail. His eyes were dark and dim. Have you heard of bright eyes? Well, I would call him dark eyes. His salt-and-pepper, unkempt, dingy beard practically hid his parched, cracked, dry black lips. And then I noticed that his limp was more like he was sort of dragging his left leg. As if he couldn't or didn't want to lift his left foot too high off the ground. Maybe his left leg had some malfunction or an affliction, or maybe that was the only way to keep his unlaced, dilapidated shoe on his foot. They, his shoes, were worn and torn and, as I said, had no strings. His clothes were dirty and stained. Really filthy and nasty.

Just as I was about to speak, he stopped—just out of arm's reach —and said, "Morning, sir. May I have one of your apples?" I knew it! I knew it! I knew it! He was coming for my apples. I knew it! That's why I was trying to avoid him. I knew it! I knew it!

Now, you know I didn't go to this store this morning to get apples. But when I saw them, they had an enchanting and alluring effect on me. And do you know what? Those apples were all I bought. They didn't have the vitamins that I had gone there to get. Neither did I find that other item, which I have forgotten what it was. All I bought was those enticing, juicy-looking, pretty, delicious red apples. Nonetheless, I left the store in high anticipation because I had my apples. High anticipation of eating my enticing, juicy-looking, pretty, delicious red apples.

Now he had asked me for one of my enticing, juicy-looking, pretty, delicious red apples. Now these were big apples too—big, pretty, enticing, delicious red apples. I mean a big handful were these apples. I looked and examined the bag of apples to determine which one I would give him. Naturally, it would be the smallest one in the bag. Even that one was a big handful of apple. So I tore open the plastic bag from the center with my right hand and grabbed the smallest apple from the middle of the bunch.

As I raised my head and my right hand with the apple in it, I noticed, just over his left shoulder, a lady leaning against the store column (tightly clutching a small child). He knew that I had seen them too. I could tell by the expression on his face. Yes, he knew. Maybe because of the expression on my face. Anyway, he knew. Without turning around, he said, "That's my wife and son," with his hand held out, reaching for the apple. Hot tears welled up in my eyes. My throat became tense and dry. I couldn't swallow. But I knew that I couldn't cry. No way! No crying!

And for some reason, from somewhere, I heard the following words; and they had to have been coming from me. What was I saying? Where were these words coming from? Why were these words coming out of my mouth? I heard me saying, "Would your wife and son like an apple too?" I definitely said those words. I must have said them from the expression of excitement he exhibited. "Oh yes, they would, sir! Thank you so very much, sir! May God truly bless you, sir!" he kept saying over and over while he was shaking my left hand so hard I thought that he would pull my arm off.

When I finally got ahold of myself and returned to reality, he was still about to shake my arm off, while I was still holding the smallest apple in the bunch in my right hand. And I looked at the bag of apples, my bag of big, pretty, juicy, enticing apples. Okay, let's see. There are three apples for them, and I'll still have three left for me plus this one still in my right hand. Yes, I was counting and contemplating my apples and noticed that he was still about to shake my left arm off in his excitement. "Thank you, sir. This will be like a whole meal."

And then it happened again. Some spirit or something got ahold of me again. And what did I hear? It made me say that. That ghost that entered my body. "A meal? What about your next meal?"

"That, sir, I don't know. I just hope and pray that the Lord will provide," he said, still elated and still shaking my hand.

Without another word, I withdrew my left hand from his hands, picked up the bag of six apples, and handed the bag of apples to him. He was shocked. He was startled. And so was I. My bag of enticing, delicious red apples. He clutched the bag of apples to his chest and held it tight and secure, like a mother would hold her child. Yes, he held the bag of apples firmly but snugly to his chest and repeatedly shouted, "Thank you, sir! May God bless you, sir!" He repeatedly thanked me as he hurried, as best as he could, toward his wife and son, all the while dragging his afflicted left leg.

I pushed my cart into the cart return area and began searching my pockets for my car keys. I then realized that I still had the smallest apple in my right hand. I switched the apple to my left hand and took the car keys from my right coat pocket, started the car, and started out the parking lot.

On my way home, I ate that apple—the smallest one in the bunch —and it was quite filling. And I was happy. I felt good. And I found myself wondering where that family was now. I didn't see them when I was leaving the parking lot. And I thought, Was I supposed to get vitamins today, or were the apples the reason I was at the store? Was this day's excursion a means to make me feel good or to provide apples for that family? Or was it both? Whatever the reason, I was happy and satisfied as I finished eating the seventh apple.

Give Me My Oscar

They pass by my house at night
And see the light
In my window
But they don't know
My pain and my plight:
That it's a candle
Burning behind the window shade
Sitting on the windowsill
Because the monies that
I recently made
Was not enough to pay
My electric bill.

So give me my Oscar
And my Tony award And my Grammy
Because I've paid my
dues. There's a gigantic smile on my face
But my heart is crushed
And my soul is singing the blues.
So don't you see?
There's no better actor than me.
So give me my Oscar and my Tony—
And my Grammy too!

She was my everything—
My sole reason to live.
And everything that I had,
To her I was willing to give.
I gave her my heart, my love, my soul.
She took them and crushed them
And lo and behold—

While attempting to cover up
My heartbreak's demise—
I lost control of my emotions
When I laughed until I cried.

So give me my Oscar
And my Tony award
And my Grammy
Because I've paid my dues.
There's a gigantic smile on my face
But my heart is crushed
And my soul is singing the blues.
So don't you see?
There's no better actor than me.
So give me my Oscar and my Tony—
And my Grammy too!

I high-five the mail carrier
Every day that he comes by.
He high-fives me back
And gives me a sigh
Because I'm always waiting there
Next to the mailbox.
There's no sole in my shoes
So I'm standing there
In my socks.
But he chats with me
For a short while
Because he knows that
My agonies have assailed.
And the both of us know that
He's only delivering bills and junk mail.

So give me my Oscar
And my Tony award
And my Grammy
Because I've paid my dues.
There's a gigantic smile on my face
But my heart is crushed
And my soul is singing the blues.
So don't you see?
There's no better actor than me.
So give me my Oscar and my Tony—
And my Grammy too!

But I'm still looking and seeking
For a tiny bit of hope.
I'm trying many different therapies
In hope that I will cope.
While they are asking,
"Are you some kind of jerk?
Why did you jump on your boss at work?"
Or "What happened to that guy in the store?"
I didn't know that I did that anymore.
He caught me off guard
When he let out that loud shout.
I just reacted as I was taught.
I didn't mean to knock him out.
Or "Your anger is out of control.
This is getting to be too much.
Why in the world would you
Choke a man in the church?"

So give me my Oscar
And my Tony award
And my Grammy
Because I've paid my dues.

There's a gigantic smile on my face
But my heart is crushed
And my soul is singing the blues.
So don't you see?
There's no better actor than me.
So give me my Oscar and my Tony—
And my Grammy too!

See, I can't live the normal life
Nor be a normal friend.
So I crawl into my foxhole
In my bedroom or my den
To live out there until my end.
With nothing to give
And no reason to live.
Nothing to lose
And nothing to win.

So give me my Oscar
And my Tony award
And my Grammy
Because I've paid my dues.
There's a gigantic smile on my face
But my heart is crushed
And my soul is singing the blues.
 So don't you see?
There's no better actor than me.
So give me my Oscar and my Tony—
And my Grammy too!

RELIGIOUS AND SPIRITUAL
INSPIRATIONS

A Rotten Apple

(Written for "Exposition of Theme" for Deacon's Alliance Program and presented at Rose of Sharon Community Church in Plainfield, New Jersey)

Giving honor to the Godhead: the Father, the Son, and the Holy Spirit. To the great pastor of this house of prayer, Reverend Millicent Ball; to all the pastors and ministers in the pulpit; to the officers of this body of Christ, as well as the officers of all other bodies represented here. And to all members, friends, and others: Good afternoon!

I want to thank Deaconess Katie Barneau for volunteering me to say a few words about the exposition of our theme, which is "Walking and Talking in the Spirit Bears Good Fruit."

Read passage: Galatians 5:16 – 23 (NIV)

[16] So I say walk by the spirit, and you will not gratify the desires of the flesh. [17] for the flesh desires what is contrary to the spirit, and the spirit what is contrary to the flesh. They are in conflict with each other, so you are not to do whatever you want. [18] but if you are led by the spirit, you are not under the law.

[19] The acts of the flesh are obvious: sexual immorality, impurity and debauchery; [20] idolatry and witchcraft; hatred, discord, jealousy, fits of rage, selfish ambition, dissensions, factions [21] and envy; drunkenness, orgies, and the like. I warn you, as I did before, that those who live like this will not inherit the kingdom of god.

[22] But the fruit of the spirit is love, joy, peace, forbearance, kindness, goodness, faithfulness, [23] gentleness, and self-control. Against such things there is no law.

State theme: "Walking and Talking in the Spirit Bears Good Fruit."

We see here in verses 16, 17, and 18 where it tells us that there is always a conflict going on between the flesh and the spirit. And we see in verses 19, 20, and 21 the lusts of the flesh. And finally, verses 22 to 23 concentrate on the good fruit that's produced from walking in the spirit.

As I thought about it and meditated on these scriptures, the more I realized that this fruit, this good fruit, is not just something that just happens. Instead, it's the product of a process.

So let's examine (briefly) what this process entails. Now where I grew up in the Mississippi Delta, almost everyone had some type of fruit tree in their yard—whether it was a peach tree, a plum tree, a pear tree, a fig tree, an apple tree, or what have you. Nonetheless, I would like to focus on just one fruit today. Let's say the apple.

Now then the question becomes, what makes the apple a good fruit? What is the process? Or what criterion goes into making that apple a good fruit? First, where does the apple come from? The tree branch or the tree? That tree is the source from where the apple obtains what it needs to become a good fruit.

The first thing that the apple tree needs is the proper amount of sunshine. The tree needs light. The sunshine is absorbed by the chlorophyll in the leaves and, through a process called photosynthesis, produces water and sugar that feed the apple.

Just like that apple tree, we need light too. Our light is Jesus Christ. A process takes place—something happens—when we let the light of Christ shine in our lives.

The lord is my light and my salvation. (Ps. 27:1a, NIV)

Let your light so shine before men, that they may see your good works and glorify your father in heaven. (Matt. 5:16, NKJV)

Then Jesus spoke to them again, saying, "I am the light of the world. He who follows me shall not walk in darkness, but have the light of life." (John 8:12, NKJV)

For we were once darkness, but now you are light in the lord. Walk as children of light (for the fruit of the spirit is in all goodness, righteousness, and truth). (Eph. 5:8–9, NKJV)

Yes, just as the apple tree needs the sunshine, we too need the light of Christ.

But that tree also needs to be in the soil. It needs to be rooted and anchored in good soil for a firm foundation. And also, the roots seek out nutrients and minerals from the ground. Do I need to say that we need to be grounded too? That we need to be grounded in the Word of God—the Bible?

But when the sun was up, they were scorched, and because they had no root they withered away. (Matt. 13:6, NKJV)

For if the first fruit is holy, the lump is also holy; and if the root is holy, so are the branches. (Rom. 11:16, NKJV)

That's where we get that succulent and sweet apple from, hanging on a limb on the tree. But if the root didn't provide its necessities, do you hear what I'm saying? If we don't have the Word in us, how grounded can we be?

Okay, we have the sunshine (the light), and we have our roots grounded in the Bible. We got it made in the shade now, don't you think? Easy sailing, huh? Don't bet on it. What about rain? Isn't rain important? Sure it is. We don't want it to rain. It makes things all sloppy and wet. It messes up my day. But that soil needs the rain. And so do you. If you never have any trials or temptations to overcome, then how will you know that you can persevere? These trials and temptations strengthen our faith and allow us to stand. To stand for the truth of God. So don't be afraid of the trials, because they will come.

Man who is born of woman is of few days and full of trouble. (Job 14:1, NKJV)

My brethren, count it all joy when you fall into various trials, knowing that the testing of you faith produces patience. (James 1:2–3, NKJV)

Blessed is the man who endures temptation; for when he has been proved, he will receive the crown of life which the lord has promised to those who love him. (James 1:12, NKJV)

Nowww! We are set! We have the proper sunshine, the proper grounding in the Word, and we are persevering through our trials. Nothing can stop us now. Right!

Well, have you ever seen a shiny, juicy-looking apple and found a worm inside? What can keep the birds from sitting on a branch and pecking holes in all the apples? What about other animals too? The fruit needs protection. That's it. And so do we. And we have it. We have it in the form of the Holy Spirit. The Holy Spirit is our protection from sin. The Holy Spirit gives us the ability to overcome sin.

But put on the Lord Jesus Christ and make no provisions for the flesh, to fulfill it lusts. (Rom. 13:14, NKJV)

I say then: walk in the spirit, and you shall not fulfill the lust if the flesh. (Gal. 5:16, NKJV)

So then with the proper amount of rain; the proper amount of nutrients from the earth or the ground; and the proper protection (in the form of the Holy Spirit) from the birds, insects, and other harmful animals, we can expect to harvest plump, pretty, juicy, sweet-tasting apples. Good fruit.

We must spend the proper amount of time reading the Word of God. Spend the proper time meditating on the Word of God. Spend the proper time on your knees, praying, talking to God. And we will produce good fruit.

Yes, walking and talking in the Spirit bears good fruit. But have you ever picked up a fruit, washed it off, shined it up, and bit into it with great anticipation? Expecting a sweet flavor in your mouth and got either a sour taste or a doty, no-flavored taste at all? Have you ever examined a fruit, expecting succulent satisfaction, only to find out that it has a worm in it? So what do we have now? It's not a good fruit. Instead, it's a rotten apple. I mean rotten to the core. And I'm sure that we all have heard that one rotten apple spoils the whole bunch.

What makes an apple a rotten apple? It's quite evident as we can see in Galatians 5:19–21.

[19] the acts of the flesh are obvious: sexual immorality, impurity and debauchery; [20] idolatry and witchcraft; hatred, discord, jealousy, fits of rage, selfish ambition, dissensions, factions [21] and envy; drunkenness, orgies, and the like. I warn you, as I did before, that those who live like this will not inherit the kingdom of God.

If you are a rotten apple, it's not too late. For God is a merciful and forgiving God. If you have fallen, don't let Satan shame you into staying a rotten apple. He will pick you up and clean you off and sanctify you. But you must be responsible.

Now you, brothers and sisters, who are so holy, would you just sit there and watch your foot rot off and do nothing? Or your hand rotting away and do nothing but talk about it? Well, Paul tells us in the twelfth chapter of 1 Corinthians that we are all one body. Christ is the head, and we make up the body of the church. So when you do nothing to lift your brother out of the mire, you are allowing a part of your own body to rot away.

First Thessalonians 5:14 (NKJV) says, "Now we exhort you, brethren, warn those who are unruly, comfort the fainthearted, uphold the weak, be patient with all."

Remember, things happen when you let the light of Christ shine in your life; when you ground yourself in the Word of God; when you allow the Holy Spirit to take control of your actions, thoughts, and deeds. And how much stronger will you be with your brother or sister in Christ there at your side? After all, Christ didn't send anyone out by himself. He sent them together or, at least, in pairs.

You don't have to be a rotten apple, and you won't if you abide by our theme, "Walking and Talking in the Spirit Bears Good Fruit." If we walk in the Spirit, we will then produce good fruit.

And I Said, "Thank You, Lord!"

I woke up this morning and rolled out of bed,
In a beautiful home with a roof over my head.
And I said, "Thank you, Lord!"

I showered and shaved and took out my clothes,
Then I dressed myself from head to toes.
And I said, "Thank you, Lord!"

I sat down to breakfast at my kitchen table
And ate heartily. I know some who're not able.
And I said, "Thank you, Lord!"

I started to work, which is quite far,
But I gave him thanks for driving a fairly decent car.
And I said, "Thank you, Lord!"

In the office bathroom, a man was singing the blues.
He was drying his shirt and running shoes.
And I said, "Thank you, Lord!"

His hair was uncombed, and his top was bald
As he continued to dry his shirt under the blower on the wall.
And I said, "Thank you, Lord!"

His clothes were wrinkled, dingy, and old.
Fall is nearly over; it soon will be cold.
Is he homeless? Does he have food to eat?
Those ragged shoes can't provide warmth for his feet.
A salt-and-pepper beard. Kinky, unkempt hair.
Next meal coming from only God knows where.
My heart sank as I continued on my way.
My, how I am blessed is what God showed me today!
How can I not praise him for what he has done?
So I humbly bow in the Spirit to the Father and the Son.
And I worship the Godhead by saying,
"Thank you, Lord! Thank you, Lord!
Thank you, Lord!" "Hallelujah! Thank you, Lord!"

Christmastime

The weather has become a risk.
The wind is blowing quite brisk
And beating like a whisk.
Christmas is on its way.

Outside my window, all is white.
Snow has fallen during the night.
Birds have already taken their flight.
Christmas is on its way.

The leaves are gone. The trees are bare.
Shoppers are darting from here to there,
Selecting gifts from everywhere.
Christmas is on its way.

Food piled on the table—high!
Neighbors and relatives stopping by.
Everyone has a friendly hi!
Christmas is on its way.

That's all well and good, and yet
There's one thing we shouldn't forget.
Christ is the one who paid the debt.
Only in him is there Christmastime.

In the Lord

Bad enough.
Sad enough.
Lord knows that I've had enough.
But I've never been glad enough
Until I found good enough
In the Lord!

Bad times.
Sad times.
Lord knows that I've had some times.
But I've never had any glad times
Until I found a good time
In the Lord!

Bad luck.
Sad luck.
Lord knows that I've had luck.
But I've never had any glad luck
Until I found good luck
In the Lord!

Bad news.
Sad news.
Lord knows that I've had some news.
But I've never had any glad news
Until I found good news
In the Lord!

My Baby's Daddy

Giving all honor and glory to the Godhead: the Father, the Son, and the Holy Ghost. To my senior pastor, Bishop Eddie Bennett Jr.; to our first lady and copastor, Dr. Yvonne Bennett; to all officials—the elders, ministers, deacons, and deaconess; to all HCF members and friends; and to anyone else that makes up the congregation, good morning and happy Black History Month.

I could stand here and spout off pages and pages of black scientists, mathematicians, inventors, kings and queens, and people of prominence, prestige, and power. But my concern and passion for today's black man and the plight and condition of many of our black families compel me to ask the question, will that really suffice?

I am so tired, so hurt, so disappointed and dismayed with the plight and conditions of many of our black families today. But focusing mainly on the black male—the black man, my brother—do you know how it grieves me to hear the words "my baby's daddy"? When I first heard that expression, I asked myself, "What kind of language is that?"

But unfortunately, that phrase seems to actually depict so many of my beloved black families today. And I am so saddened by that fact. So I find myself saying, "My brothers, grow up and be a man."

Oh, how I appreciate HCF's Men's Fellowship Ministry, where we discuss being better men for God by being better husbands and better fathers. My wife, Audrey, can tell you how excited I get as the date of our meeting approaches. These meetings are important because of the dire need for instructions on being a man. For:

When I was a child, I talked like a child, I thought like a child, I reasoned like a child. When I became a man, I put childish ways behind me. (1 Cor. 13:11, NIV)

It is not good to have zeal without knowledge, nor to be hasty and miss the way. (Prov. 19:2, NIV)

My people are destroyed for lack of knowledge: because thou hast rejected knowledge, I will also reject thee, that thou shalt be no priest to me: seeing thou hast forgotten the law of thy God, I will also forget thy children. (Hosea 4:6, KJV)

Yes, this type of thinking hurts us for generations to come. So I'm glad that in these meetings, we learn what we need to do to be a man, not a "baby's daddy." This is like me being a farmer—just finding any spot of soil and throwing the seed on the ground and then continuing on my way. I didn't test the soil to see if it was good soil or not. I didn't check to see if the seed was covered or not. I didn't till the soil around the seed. I didn't water the soil nor fertilize the soil to ensure that my seed got the proper water and nutrients to grow up strong and healthy. I didn't cultivate the soil to make sure that my seed would not be surrounded by toxic weeds.

But since there is so much immorality, each man should have his own wife, and each woman her own husband. (1 Cor. 7:2, NIV)

It says husband and not "my baby's daddy." It makes me want to scream, "My brother, grow up and be a man!"

But if any provide not for his own, and especially for those of his own house, he hath denied the faith, and is worse than an infidel. (1 Tim. 5:8, KJV)

Oh, I understand that you want to seem macho. You are looking for a way to prove your masculinity. To that end, I say, "Come to Christ and be saved and delivered. Let the Word of God be your role model even if there are others there in the natural."

Yes, find your masculinity in the Lord, not in being a baby's daddy. My brother, grow up and be a man. I penned a few words depicting my masculinity some time ago in the form of a verse, a poem. And I entitled this piece "Masculinity at Its Finest," and I would like to share it with you, if I may.

(Read poem.)

Masculinity at Its Finest

Do you know what time I went to bed last night?

Seven! That's right, seven.
Do you know what time I went to sleep?
Eleven! That's right, eleven.
Four hours I lay there,
    Thinking of hell and heaven.
Hell, that's right, and heaven.
I'm a man, and there are few of us.
Compared to women, we're one to seven.
One, that's right, to seven.
There's a woman for every day of the week.
And you can find them if you'll only seek.
There's one for Monday, Tuesday, Wednesday,
Thursday, Friday, Saturday, and Sunday—
A different lady to make every night a fun day.
All night long, allow her to
    Hug you, squeeze you, and kiss you.
Leave here saturated with infatuation,
    Not knowing that for a week, she'll miss you.
Change them like you do your underwear—
    A different one each day.
Lead them on and use them.
You know what to do and say.
So go on, man, and grab you one.
Grab, that's right, you one.
And have some fun.
Thaaaat's right, you son-of-a-gun.
Even if your week increases to thirteen days,
    Don't worry about enough ladies:
They'll keep on having babies.
But if they stop having babies,
    You can have my entitled six.
Now don't think for a moment
    That I'll be in a fix.
Encircled in a woman's arms,

I know that's heaven to you.
Encircled in a woman's arms
    Is heavenly. I know that's true.
Encircled in a woman's arms
    Is heaven to me too.
But if one woman wants to hold me
    Every night of the week, then
        For me, one woman will do.
One woman, that's right, for me will do.
As many women as you can get
    Is a lesson for you to heed.
But one woman who really loves me
    Is all I need.
One woman, that's right, who really loves me
    Is all I need.

So, my brothers, I'm sure that if you are in Christ, then that too will be your mantra of masculinity. We should never be satisfied just being a "baby's daddy." We need to be real men. We need to be fathers. We need to be husbands. So I beg you with all my heartfelt love and compassion that I have for you from the greatest depths of my heart and soul, "Grow up and be a man!"

Please, Lord, Forgive Me

Please, Lord, forgive me!

I went to church today. And the pastor's sermon was still in my head.
When I ran into a traffic jam, you should have heard the words that I said.
I was confronted by the person in the car next to me.
None of us could go anywhere. I'm sure that he could see.
So he said some things to me that I really didn't like.
So I told him—to put it nicely—to go and take a hike.
After a short back-and-forth conversation,
There arose in my spirit a certain revelation.
And that sensation—that's what I'm calling it now—
Made me think of blessed quietness instead of a "powwow."
So, Lord, my heart became heavy and forlorn.
And it was that sensation that made me feel that I was wrong.
And when I came to my spiritual senses, it grieved my heart so much
That I feel as if I am asking you to forgive me for going to church.

So, Lord, I'm coming to you truthfully. And, Lord, this is it.
Lord, I just want to be your servant and not some old hypocrite.

Please, Lord, forgive me!

I read your Word this morning—aloud.
Later I was out shopping, and, Lord, what a crowd.
There were people running, elbowing, and pushing.
And there I was frustrated, stagnated, and wishing
That these people would go somewhere: jump in the lake.
I could go poof! and make them disappear if that's what it would take.
They didn't care about anyone else.
The whole aisle they thought was theirs.
They stopped and were standing there with their carts filled with their wares.
I couldn't go around nor backward nor through.
And, Lord, I know that it was wrong what I decided to do.
So I got angry and said some words. And, Lord, I know you heard.
And, Lord, I feel like I'm asking your forgiveness for me reading your Word.
So, Lord, I'm coming to you truthfully. And, Lord, this is it.
Lord, I just want to be your servant and not some old hypocrite.

Please, Lord, forgive me!

I prayed to you—humbly, I thought—while down on my knees.
And I asked that you let me make it through this day sinless, please.
Lord, I wanted badly to be a good representative for you
In all the things that I would say and all the things that I would do.
And, lo and behold, I ran across—let's just say—a friend.
Who happened to be someone that I should've avoided to the end.
So he stopped me. He got my attention.
He immediately started complaining. Oh, the things he did mention.
I pretended that I was interested in the things that he was saying.
But, Lord, all the while, your Word I was disobeying.
I was not interested in what he was saying, spewing out all that gossip.
Lord, I was wrong. I should have stopped him when it first rolled off his lips.
And, Lord, I knew that I was wrong in not doing what I was supposed to.
It seems that I am asking your forgiveness, almost, for praying to you.

So, Lord, I'm coming to you truthfully. And, Lord, this is it.
Lord, I just want to be your servant and not some old hypocrite.

Please, Lord, forgive me!

In reality, I'm not asking your forgiveness for going to church,
Even though not applying what I had heard pains me very much.
And I'm not asking forgiveness for reading your Word or the prayers I prayed.
But, Lord, it's that I wasn't mature enough; and in that I strayed.
It pains me that I can go to church, read your Word, pray, and still
Not allow your Spirit to guide my heart, which causes me to do your will.
So, Lord, I pray for your forgiveness and that from me you'll never part.
So make your Word and your Spirit live not in my head but in my heart.

So, Lord, I'm coming to you truthfully. And, Lord, this is it.
Lord, I just want to be your servant and not some old hypocrite.

Practice What I Preach

Lord, let me hold your hand
    As I stagger from day to day,
    Trying my best to walk in
    A child of Christlike way.
Lord, let me touch your fingertips
    Each and every time I reach;
    And, Lord, most of all,
    Let me practice what I preach.

Lord, let me walk in your footsteps
    With your Spirit as my eyes
    So that in your Word and way,
    I, too, may become wise.
Lord, I seek your Spirit so
    That about it I can teach.
    And, Lord, most of all,
    Let me practice what I preach.

Lord, let me be your temple—
    My whole body and soul.
    And that I may be an example for
    Some lost sinner to behold.
Lord, let me be your light
    And not old Satan's leech.
    And, Lord, most of all, I pray,
    Let me practice what I preach.

Son of Purity

From the day of my conception,
I—me,
    My heart,
    My thoughts,
    My mind, all of me—
Was shaped in iniquity
And shaped in sin and shame.

Darkness surrounded and lived
In my heart,
    My mind, and
    My thoughts.
Hatred, Envy,
Anger, and
Violence were my claim to fame.

But he took the towelette
    Of his love
And dampened it in my warm tears,
As he gently
    But passionately
        Washed my soul.

He cleansed me
    Without and within
    From a dirty,
    Filthy
Sinner of darkness
To a bright and
    Alluring
        Son of purity.

(A Visit From) The Guest

Let me start out by saying that I am truly blessed,
Especially since I've been such a pest
And have made my life and others' such a mess.
Oh, I walked around drumming my chest—
Yes, full of vigor and full of zest.
I traveled north, south, east, and west,
Just daring anyone to step up to the test.
And while I was on this quest,
I had a visit from a most excellent guest,
Who convinced me that it would be best—
If I wanted to escape that deadly nest
Of damnation, turmoil, and eternal unrest—
To place my hand beneath my vest
And acknowledge the heart beating within my breast
And cry out to him who can give me rest.
And that is Christ—the Lord of lords.
That is Jesus—the Redeemer of my soul.
He is the son of God—the King of kings.
The wonderful Counselor who has made me whole.

The Resurrection

I observed this small child standing at the corner of this huge brick building. She kept peeking her head around the corner and pulling it back. She had run ahead of her mother so that she would be the first to look around the corner. The child seemed a little puzzled and a bit disappointed. While she kept peeking her head around the corner and pulling it back, she called out to her mother, as her mother was walking closer to her by now, "Mom, I don't see it! I don't see it!"

"You don't see what, honey?"

"Easter!" the child replied. "Didn't you say Easter was just around the corner?"

Well, there's one thing for sure. We are not puzzled. And we definitely are not disappointed. Yes, the Easter buzz is in the air. Can't you feel it? It's the resurrection! Yes, the resurrection of Jesus the Christ!

Come! Come with me for a moment. Let's go back into time a little over two thousand years ago. It's early Sunday morning, just about sunrise, where Peter and the other disciples (except Judas and Thomas) are locked away in this room. And there comes a knock at the door.

Knock! Knock! Knock!

"Hey! Quiet! Didn't you here that?"

"Yes, someone is knocking on the door." "But who could that be?"

"It's probably Mary and the other women."

"No! It can't be them. They went to anoint Jesus's body. They couldn't have done it this quickly. You know we must be very careful. That could be one of our persecutors. They killed Jesus, and they want to kill anyone associated with him and anyone who followed him."

Again, there was a knock at the door.

Knock! Knock! Knock!

"Ask who it is." "Who is it?"

"It sounds like the women, but they can't be finished anointing the body this quickly."

"Who is it?"

She said, "Mary. Open the door."

He opens the door and let Mary and Mary Magdalene and the other women into the room.

"Why are you all back so soon? Did you anoint the body that fast?" "No! His body was not there!"

"What do you mean the body was not there?"

"His body was not there. At first, we thought someone had stolen our Lord's body."

"Stolen the Lord's body?"

"No, no, no! We thought someone had. After we looked into the tomb and his body was not there, we turned around. And there was this big, bright, blinding light. It was an angel."

"An angel?"

"It had to be. And we were frightened!" "Well, what happened?"

"He told us not to be afraid. And then he asked us who we were looking for."

"Did you tell him? Did you tell him?"

"Yes. We told him that we were looking for our Lord Jesus. That we came to anoint his body with oil and spices. And he said the strangest thing."

"What did he say? What did he say?"

"He asked us why we were seeking the living among the dead."

"The living among the dead? Something's not right here. I've got to find my Lord's body. I'm going to the tomb myself. Is anybody going with me? We must hurry."

Running. Huffing and puffing.

"I know that his body has to be there. Maybe they looked in the wrong tomb. If he's there, I'll find him. I'll find my Lord's body.

Whew! We're here. There's the tomb. But where's the body?" "Do you think someone stole the body?"

"No! No one would have stolen the body and left the shroud. And folded it so nice and neatly. Look!"

"Do you think that maybe he just got up walked out?"

"No! He was dead! I witnessed it. I witnessed every grueling, painful detail of his suffering."

"Yes, I witnessed it too. He was dead!"

"I too witnessed his suffering and his death."

"I too was there. I was there Thursday night when he went to the Garden of Gethsemane on the Mount of Olives to pray. I was there until after midnight—into early Friday morning—when they came and arrested him. I was there after his seventh trial where the Roman soldiers mocked him and tortured him. They pushed a crown of thorns upon his head. The thorns cut his flesh, and blood ran down his face. I was there when they made him carry his cross up the hill. That was the most painful and gut-wrenching noon that I have ever witnessed. I can still hear the ringing sound of the hammer as it struck the nails that penetrated his hands and feet. I was there when they crucified him and when that soldier took his big, long spear and jabbed it into his side. I was there when the blood and water came gushing out. I was there when Joseph of Arimathea, Nicodemus, and the others placed his limp body right here in this grave. In this tomb right here. Yes, he was dead! And yet he's not here!"

"Hey, this is the third day. Do you remember what he told the Jews in the temple? He said, 'If you destroy this temple in three days, I will raise it up again.' Do you think that's what this means? Maybe he has risen!"

"You may be right! It was prophesied that he would bear our griefs and sorrows and that he would be wounded and bruised for our sins, and by his

stripes, we are healed."

"Yes! Yes! Yes! I can see it too now. That's what he meant when he said 'And they shall scourge him and put him to death, and on

the third day, he will rise again.'"

"And I recall what he said to the Pharisees, telling them that as Jonah was three days and three nights in the belly of a huge fish, so the son of man will be three days and three nights in the heart of the earth. Do you remember that?"

"Yes! And I remember what he said before he rebuked me by saying,

'Get thee behind me, Satan.' He said that he must go to Jerusalem, suffer many things, and be killed and be raised again on the third day."

There is no other answer. He has risen! Jesus has risen from the dead. Hallelujah! Our Christ has risen! Our Lord has risen! Will you praise him with me? Hallelujah! He has risen! Hallelujah! He has risen! Hallelujah! He has risen! Hallelujah! He has risen!

HEALING WOUNDS – INSPIRATION, COPING, AND RECOVERY

A Euphoric Moment

There have been a lot of talk, a lot of research, and a lot of rationalization concerning veterans' suicides lately. I think that it's a good thing that they/we are talking about it (depending on what we're saying, if we are doing something about it). It's good that they are willing to research the reasons of these tragic occurrences, but what are we going to do about it? In all actuality, these occurrences, as numerous as they are, validate themselves; and that's a shame.

Isn't it ironic? A soldier can (and will) travel to faraway, foreign lands. They can (and will) utilize the wiles of learned survival training to stay alive, even to the extent of taking the lives of others when— at least if they think it's so—it's necessary. Yes, how ironic it is to be so physically fit that you can kill someone with your bare hands, but until you are mentally controlled, you can't hurt a fly. It's all now instinctive. No thoughts necessary. I am a soldier, a killer, an emotionally trained killer.

Parenthetically, I think it's important—very, very important—to mention (at this time) that there's a vast difference between a *killer* and a murderer. Something deep within me finds it a necessity to mention that. Something deep down in my soul must speak it, say it, hear it, and believe it. Yes, there's a vast moral difference, I think. I believe.

Okay! Okay! Okay! Back to the topic at hand. Now what were we talking about? Oh yes, veterans' suicides. Uh, more death. More death talk.

Anyhow, we do what we are trained to do. We are loyal. We are dependable and able. And (if I must say so myself) we are damn good at it. Unfortunately, sometimes the killings become the end-all result of the mission, and that's not all right. As if to say that other killings are okay. Maybe morally okay.

Oh yes, veterans' suicides. We don't have to think; we just react, so to speak, because there's that constant voice of rote training that's screaming loudly inside our heads. But of course, the voices are not the problem. The problem is in the switch—the switch that turns off the voices. The switch is flipped and flipped and flipped, but the voices don't stop. And that's what makes one angry. I'm not upset (I mean angry; no, I really mean *mad, damn mad!*) with the voices, but with the switch that turns them off. So now they are always there. Always loud! Always shouting and screaming! This noise just won't go away. No peace! No peace! No peace! Just a moment of peace! Where's the peace when the switch doesn't work?

Sure, I've thought about it. You know, suicide. But I know that I could never do it. How could I kill ... me? No way! No how! And until now, I could not see how anyone else could. Of course, I could reason why, but until that day, I could not see it so plainly.

I had just left the VA and was driving home. I had the windows down and was cruising about seventy-five or eighty miles per hour down the highway. The radio was blasting away. The wind was blowing in my ears and swirling around inside the car. The swirling and force of the air shut out all other outside noises and mentally lifted me into some wonderful, peaceful place.

Oh, what a place! Not a care! Oh, what peace! My mind had drifted into this peaceful palace. I drifted into this wonderful, peaceful palace of euphoria. If only I could stay in this peaceful place forever. I shall not go back to that world of noise and confusion. Oh, what peace!

Then I was jolted back by a shield or curtain of black, and I found myself rapidly approaching the tailgate of a huge eighteen-wheeler.

Damn! I thought because I knew that I was back. And that made me mad, damn mad.

I'm back. No more peaceful place. And in that peaceful place is where I wanted to be ... to stay. My mind wanted that peace, and some badly. We—my mind and me—decided that if I just gunned the accelerator a bit, we could permanently make it to that peaceful place.

That's our decision! That's what we'll do! And as we sent the command, my right foot became a trembling traitor as it lightly tapped the brakes.

Just a few feet from the tractor trailer (and near that peaceful place), the car began decreasing its speed. The distance between us —the truck and that peaceful place—grew wider and wider.

I was there—almost. I was almost there in that peaceful place. That was my chance. I can't commit suicide, and I have a trembling, traitorous right foot to prove it. No, I can't do it. But for the first time, due to my *euphoric* moment, I can see why someone else would, especially my veteran comrades. God, please help their switches work against the voices and their shouting, screaming noises.

LOVE, ROMANCE, AND SUCH

A Missed Opportunity

It was sort of quiet that morning
In the car while I was driving her to work.
The radio was playing.
 And a little conversation.
 Somehow it seemed quiet to me.
Maybe it was in my mind.
 You think?
But I felt that it was there. I sensed it.

 We had spoken a few sentences toward each other,
And the tone was not a tone of endearment, shall I say.
 Maybe it was just me.
But I ache—my heart does,
 When those things happen.
Yes, it pulls and tears at my heartstring
 When someone, especially someone
 Whom I love so dearly and so deeply,
Has been treated harshly.

 Sure, it might have been only in my mind.
Maybe it was just my feelings of guilt
Controlling my mind and my mood and
My thoughts and my feelings and my thinking.
Controlling me.
 But nonetheless,
I felt the need to rectify the situation,
The need to seek peace and forgiveness.
I needed to do something to extract that bright,
Brilliant, beautiful smile that lay
Just beneath the surface
Of my wife's gorgeous and lovely facade.

 Yes, I must do something ...
But what? You know,

Even if there was nothing there,
Even if it was only in my mind,
I must do something. But what, Roy?
What? Think? What?

Aha! Yeah! Okay! Okay! Yes!
Yes! That's it. When I pick her up
From work this evening,
I'll be standing there
at the bottom of the courthouse steps.
You know how the limo drivers have those signs
With their client's name on them?
That's what I'll do.
I'll have a sign that says,
"My darling wife, your limo awaits."

Yes! That's what I'll do.
I'll have the darling card or sign in one hand,
And in my right hand,
I'll have an extra-long-stemmed (just one) pink carnation
But surrounded by—you know,
Around the stem area,
Surrounded by—lively lilac,
Purple, bluish ...
What color were they?
Yeah! Surrounded by lively,
Smiling forget-me-nots.

Yeah, she'll like that. I know that pink
Is one of her favorite colors, and
The forget-me-nots are akin to a purplish color.
Oh yes, she'll like that. That'll make her smile.
And at the end of a long, hard day's work too.
A long-stemmed pink carnation
Surrounded by forget-me-nots.

Oh no, look at the time! I'm already late.

I didn't Finish my task on time. Now I'm stuck
In this bumper-to-bumper traffic.
What do I do? Do I make myself later
By trying to find a flower shop? Or
Do I just keep going?
What do I do?

     Hey, there's a flower shop
In that little strip mall ahead. Aw, shucks!
It's closed. Darn it!

     Well, will there be a quiet ride
In the car this evening on our way home?
Can I get this out of my head?
Out of my mind? Can I pretend
That these thoughts of an attempt
To make her smile never happened?

     Intentions! My intentions!
An opportunity that has passed me by.
I can't say anything. How can I say
I intended to ... I feel like
The minister who skipped church
To play golf on Sunday. Now he has
No one to tell that he made a hole in one.
Who's he going to tell?

     Do you know why I feel so bad?
So guilty? So ashamed? I squandered away
A great opportunity. A great opportunity!
An opportunity to make my wife,
The woman of my dreams: my wife,
The love of my life: my wife,
One of the greatest blessings
That the Lord has bestowed upon me.
And I missed a great opportunity
To make her smile. Wow!

A Conversation with a Friend

Man, this must be the
Heaviest picture album that
I have ever seen. It's
Packed with pictures
Of beautiful women.

Are you kidding me?
You could not have met
That many beautiful girls.
They are all fine and sexy too.

Oh yes, I like that jacket.
Which one did you say
Gave it to you?
The one whose picture is
Sitting on the right.
My, my, my!
She's beautiful!
That watch too?

Man, she must really love you.
Wow! Look at all those cards!
Ohhhhh! I see.
A collection from
All those lovely women
That you have met.
And only the most outstanding ones!
Gosh! I wish I was in your place,
Getting all those cards,
Meeting all those women,
Receiving all those gifts.

What do you mean by
"What can the pictures and
Gifts and cards do for you?"

Are they not proof that
Those women love you?
Oh yes, I see what you mean.
And yes, I would rather
Have the woman in my arms
Than a chest full of cards.

Since you put it that way,
Sure, I would rather have
The woman. Yes, give me that woman
To be at my side.

A Need to Know

You tell me I'm your all and all.
You hint about this and that.
You make it clear where I should be
And where to hang my hat.

You tell of nobodies.
You tell me of nowhere,
Though I ask, but only get a start.
My faults are yours.
And you gladly accept your shares,
But there's a hidden place in your heart.

You look at other men and speak,
But I should have no fear,
For wherever I happen to be,
You'll soon be coming near.

You'll sacrifice the la dee da,
And I believe that it will last.
You're ready to give your life to me—
All except your past.

It causes a dreaded fear sometimes
To think that I can love you so.
Yet I could never love you as much
As someone whom I really did know.

Almost All the Women Love Me

Almost all the women love me.
I'm so natural,
  So true.
I'm so conversational,
  So honest, and
  So smooth
That almost all the women love me.

Yeah, almost all the women love me—.
I'm so me.
I'm so you.
I'm so easy
And so easy to dream of.
I'm so dramatic that
Almost all the women love me.

I know almost all the women love me
Because it's my fate.
I'm so loved.
I'm so hated.
  I'm so up
That I'm so late.
  I'm so wanting
That I'm only.
  I'm so believable
That I'm lonely.
And almost all the women love me.

I Looked at Her

I looked at her
> (sitting in my house
>> with a beautiful smile,
>>> though quiet as a mouse).

I got up,
> went over,
>> and said
>> (as I placed my hand upon her head),
"Stay here with me tonight.
> I'll start some music
>> and soften the light.

"We'll be free
> in the nude
to walk.
We'll have the privacy
> if we want to talk

"About
> if you will
>> and
> why you won't,
> how you do
>> and
> when you don't.

"We'll get high
> (if you prefer,
>> just mellow),
and
> roll among my sheets
>> of golden yellow.

"We'll holler and groan
>> and
> squeal and moan.

"We'll hiss and snatch
        and
    whisper and scratch
        and
    pinch and hold
        and
    caress and roll.

"We'll sweat and shudder and grin,
get tired,
    rest,
        and
    do it
        again.
"You say you want to
        but
    you can't:
I say you won't
    the reason you ain't.

"You say you may
    some other day.
When there's nothing else to do,
    then you'll stay,
    spend the night,
        and
roll in the hay;
laugh and grin and play,
        but
in some other way
        on
some other day.

"Well, that's okay.
    I still think you're groovy,
    but right now,
        I have a date
            to take
    my girlfriend to a movie."

Happiness Is ...

Happiness is an involuntary, wry smile,
  Stemming from my sputtering,
        Fluttering heart
  That suffers the aches
        Of writhing pain
  When we are apart.

Happiness is a swiftly falling tear
  From my adrenaline overflowing—
  As I grasp the unlimited heavens
  And pull them toward me,
        Knowing
  That it's not the heavens
        Moving at all—
    From a tug so extremely small
  But that it's me
        Growing
    And getting closer to you
        By showing.
And it's all because of *love*!
  But ahh ...
    Love's all because of *you*!

My Color

You are sweet.
I like your style.
I'd enjoy having
You around for a while.

You are gorgeous.
I am lonesome.
You are beautiful.
I am in love.

You are intelligent.
I am as you.
You are fascinating.
I am true.

You are sexy.
You are desire.
I am in need.
I am on fire.

Your eyes are gems
Of enchanting charms.
I am weak
When I'm in your arms.

Your kindness is important.
My presence is too.
But when your color is invisible,
My color is blue.

She Takes This

She takes this.
She takes that.
    And a tear develops In her eye.
I can't say
That I won't hurt her,
    But it wouldn't be .
Because I'd try.

Please Unpack

We used to giggle and laugh.
We used to sit and have our talks.
We used to hold hands and kiss
In the park while taking long walks.
We used to stroll up the hill
Until there were troubles
Trying to pay the bill.
We got nervous and really mad
And decided to take a pill.
Here's a whole bottleful to swallow
Before our fall or a spill.
We tried to pool our monies
From time to time,
But we didn't have enough nickels.
And we came up
Way short on dimes.
We started with a hug every morning
And with a snuggle every night.
Now it's "Put up your dukes!"
Wow! What a fight!
No more kind words.
Well, just a few—
None from me and seldom from you.
We use looks that cut
And words that bite,
Silence that drowns and
Kills the love light.
I know that I've been disagreeable,
And I know that it makes you pout.
But I think that we can change it.
I think that we can work it out.
I don't want you going out there.
I want you to come back.
No, I don't want you to leave;
So, honey, please unpack!

Queen of Hearts

It's said that life's a game of chance
    Like everything else on earth,
So we shuffle the deck to enhance
    The gamble of its worth.

We get deuces to be the devil
    And sevens to win or lose.
Trouble three times the normal level
    And eight times too much booze.

Four times nothing is too much for a loan
    And nines can't play the fiddle.
Fives are all right when all others are gone
    And tens those of the middle.

Sixes are just to take up spaces
    And jacks are used by all.
With aces, you win in all the places
    And kings too have a ball.

There's a card that I didn't mention—
    And one of much acclaim.
A card that deserves much attention
    And yes, Queen's the name.

There's one of mean representation—
    As mean as she can be.
I can say with no hesitation
    That Queen of Club's not for me.

The impenetrable Queen of Spades
    Is unbeatable without a doubt,
But in this world full of charades,
    She too is out.

The Queen of Diamonds has a great majority
    Of cravings more than health.

But a feeling within me takes the seniority
    That money's not always wealth.

There's the Queen that brings a smile of joy
    And love that never parts.
Since I met you, I'm a happy boy
    For you're my Queen of Hearts.

She Would

It suddenly rumbled—
    Surfaced ...
He sat there motionless, quiet
    (On a visual perception),
        But did you see his mental commotion?
        That rambling mind?
        Those subconscious thoughts?

It made him shudder mentally,
    As it smoothly oozed into control
        And shaped the crystal reaction
        That was to come ...

He would hear it from someone,
    What hospital?
    What room?
        When did she go?
        What time?
        How did she get there?
        These questions he would ask inquisitively ...

She would awaken from a long, restful sleep
    To be surprised
        By the gayest, heartwarming, most inspiring
        Bouquet of flowers,
        Sitting just out of her reach.

Slowly dropping her sights
    To the base of the vase,
        She noticed a small greeting envelope
        That was partly concealed by a picture.

Vague!
    The picture was vague!
        Unclear,
        And he flashed across her mind.
        Oh no, it couldn't be him, she thought.
But hoping
    Or just suspenseful?
        But eager,

And she pushed on the nurse's buzzer
       Rapidly and continuously.

In a voice of settling relief,
       She sighed to the immediate appearance
              Of the inquisitive nurse.
"Who sent those flowers?"

He flashed across her mind again
       As she,
              Almost trembling,
              Slowly
Took the card and picture
From the nurse's steady hands,
Who noticed her beaming smile.

It was a picture of him!
              Him!
       She reached and gently cuddled
       Her newly born offspring,
       Staring momentarily
              At that so intimate part of her
              And gazed again
                     At his picture.

It was every spit of him.
       He stood there, in his picture, casual
       (And in his casual wear)
              With his arms outstretched.

She gently closed her eyes and
       Slowly rested the picture of him upon her chest
              After reading the inscription
       Written across the picture.

Looking at the picture of him,
       She had read,
              "Take me back into your arms."
And she would.
Conjuring up a vision
Of his hopeful return,
Without hesitation, she knew that she would.
Yes, oh yes, she would.

The Conqueror

I'm not a six-foot-six giant:
I'm only five feet ten.
I'm not a big, muscular guy
Bad enough to handle ten men.
I've never studied the art of judo.
I've never taken karate either.
Asked about a bodybuilding course
And still I'd have to say neither.
I'm a domestically inclined person—
Really a peace-loving guy.
But if you want to be in one piece tomorrow,
Stop giving my girl that eye.

I'm a long way from an Adonis.
I'm probably not handsome at all.
Very seldom will you see me all dressed up,
Like I'm going to a fashion ball.
I don't have the cash to take her
To expensive places in town,
But I refuse to sit in my seat
And let you make me feel like a clown.
As I said, I'm a peace-loving man
And sure don't want to fight.
But I want to warn you here and now
That she's my woman tonight.

Oh, I've seen your big, wide brim,
Your diamond ring and velvet vest.
It's a fact that when I look at you,
I know that I'm not dressed the best.
I know your car is long and shiny,
Runs fast though smooth as a cloud,
While mine is old and sometimes dirty,
Spits and sputters and sometimes loud.
You've used your money and *Playboy lines*
Trying to take this woman from me,
But she has now what you didn't offer—
She's found *love*, you see?

The Ring

A lady gave me something today
That many women would be proud of.
Something they'd be glad to receive
As a token of eternal love.

You know what I'm referring to—
It's round and shiny and gold.
It goes along with something blue,
Something new and something old.

Don't try and spare my feelings.
She's already clipped my wing.
Sure, you're right, my dear friend,
She returned my engagement ring.

Many less women have gotten a ring,
Those who have longed for one.
But I'll be darned if today
Mine wasn't returned.

The Two of Us

We're two of a kind as sure as we are born.
We both are even Capricorns.
We both are striving, ambitious youths.
We admire each other, and that's the truth.
You head your class, and I lead mine.
Often we talk for quite some time.
I never miss a class, and neither do you.
When I enter the library, you're there too.
We're both looking for fortune and fame.
Yes, our hopes are nearly the same.
We're searching for the very same thing—
The joy and happiness that love can bring.
A wonderful relationship between man and wife,
And someone to hold as long as there's life.
A few little kids in a house of our own
To watch them grow until they're grown.
One day we'll discuss the feelings we had
When they first say "Mom!" and "Dad!"
We're two of a kind.
We have the same dreams.
We should be together.
That's the way it seems.
We have many things in common—me and you,
Though sometimes we share a different point of view.
We agree on many things, disagree on most.
Still I think we're best from coast to coast.
Many obstacles have been in our way,
But they're minor if together we stay.

I know not whether our paths shall part.
But I must say this for it's in my heart,
"If ever you'd leave, I'd be climbing the wall
But thankful of the joy. Some have none at all."

There Is a Pain in My Heart

There is a pain in my heart,
And it just won't go away.
It remains there as a void—just out of sight.
It hasn't been there from the start,
But it resides there night and day.
And it wrings out my tears whether it's day or night.

There's a burden in my soul
That lies heavily on my chest,
And it's crushing all the life out of me.
This dark cloud has taken hold
And just won't let me rest,
Like a ship that's lost and tossed on a moonless sea.

Those Things about You

Since I couldn't get you off my mind,
I decided to drop you a thoughtful line.
I miss those beautiful and sexy eyes,
Those shapely, soft, feminine thighs;
Your luscious breasts; your sunshine grin;
That aura of joviality that you live in;
The way you sway those sexy hips;
And yes, your lips—your voluptuous lips.
I have found that I shall never regret
Those things about you that I can't forget.

When She First Told Me

Some Mississippi pump water has a nasty taste
That, when you drink it,
Gives you the feeling in your body
And taste in your soul like you are
Kissing a wet, mangy dog.
And it's very heavy.
It hits the bottom of your stomach
With the thud of a three-hundred-pound overweight man
Falling to the floor
From a seventeen-foot ceiling.
It sort of gives you a sickening,
Nauseating feeling.
That's the way I felt
When she first told me.

Just imagine the rumblings
And tumbling of the ore
And gases and raw materials
As they twist and whirl
In the almost unimaginable heat
Of the lava in a ready-to-erupt volcano.
That's the way my innards felt,
Giving a feeling of heartburn and angina.
That's the way I felt—within my
Chest and stomach as fluids and bile
Boiled and swirled
And flowed vibrantly—
When she first told me.

My face and cheeks must have
Looked as saturated as the rocky
Walls of Niagara Falls,
With its constant flowing of its
Powerful liquid that flowed

And drenched everything in its path.
That's the way my tears
Propelled down my cheeks
When she first told me.

Like the tension on the surface of the blimp
Or a hot-air balloon
Or a grossly overinflated inner tube,
About to explode at any minute,
Was the feeling in my heart.
It felt—my aching, breaking heart did—
Like it would explode and cave in (both at the same time) from
The turbulent pressure of the pain
When she first told me.

Yes, I was devastated,
And I knew that
Even if I didn't die,
I could no longer live
When she first told me.
I was so hurt, and the pain
Was so great that even if
I kept breathing and walking
With blood still flowing throughout
My veins, I might as well have lain down—dead.
For I was sure that I would not be
Able to call that living.
Oh my, how it hurt when she first told me.
I never thought that I would ever
See this day
When she first told me
That she was leaving me for another.

You Walked In

You walked into my heart
And made yourself my wife
And we can call that by a variety of names.

But now we are apart
Because you walked out of my life
And I'm depending on my tears to drown out the painful flames.

Game, Set, Match

Man, let me tell you how it really hurts
When you love so deeply
And the relationship doesn't work.
You do all you can.
You give all you got.
But you get nothing in return, except a lot
Of "he said, she said" and "if I were you"
Advice telling me what I should do.
I know that she treats me wrong
Even though I know that I'm a good catch.
But when she bats those beautiful brown eyes at me,
It's game, set, match.

I said that I'd never do another good deed
When she took advantage of me.
She came in and took all I had.
She robbed me literally.
She took all my material possessions,
Especially those that I dearly wanted to hold.
She also took my heart along
While ripping out my mind and soul.
I had to renew my mind and soul,
Like growing a brand-new batch.
But she came in again
And whispered those sweet nothings.
And it was game, set, match.

So never again will she take
My kindness for a weakness.
Never again will I be deceived
By her alluring sensations of her
False and potential sweetness.
I'm going to bolt down
All my feelings for her.

I'm going to cage up my heart and emotions.
Yes, I'm going to have to secure them tightly
And fence in all my future notions.
I'm going to have to screw them down safely
And keep them chained here
Under lock and key and latch.
Because I know that the next time
That her voluptuous lips touch mine,
It's going to be game, set, match.

Fallen Angel

I feel neglected and rejected,
    Restless and lonely,
    And it seems just yesterday, I heard you say
    That you loved me only.
You have taken my heart
    Into the air,
    And from a tiny, little Delicate thread,
    You left it hanging there.
I longed for someone to hold—
    Someone to steady
    My frantic appeals.
    But you snipped the string:
    I know how a fallen angel feels.

Yesterday I was on top of the world,
    Submerged and showered with praise.
    But today I struggle to hide
    The fact that I'm empty inside,
    Like wandering around in a maze.
    I cherished your love.
    Your all, Your being.
    Blindly, I followed,
    Never seeing.
Thus, in darkness, I hung
    And gently swung,
    Caught and tied by the heels;
    And you cut that rope of love:
    I know how a fallen angel feels.

Though I'm trying my best
    To withstand the test— If you should ask
    About my task—
    It's a hurting struggle nonetheless.
I know that I'll break through

This gloomy hue—
That I don't doubt at all.
But my heart says, "I dare you!
I dare you again to fall!"
So I must keep in mind
Never be blind
And hearts don't make deals.
You know not the time of a break in the line:
And I know how a fallen angel feels.
Yes, I know how a fallen angel feels.